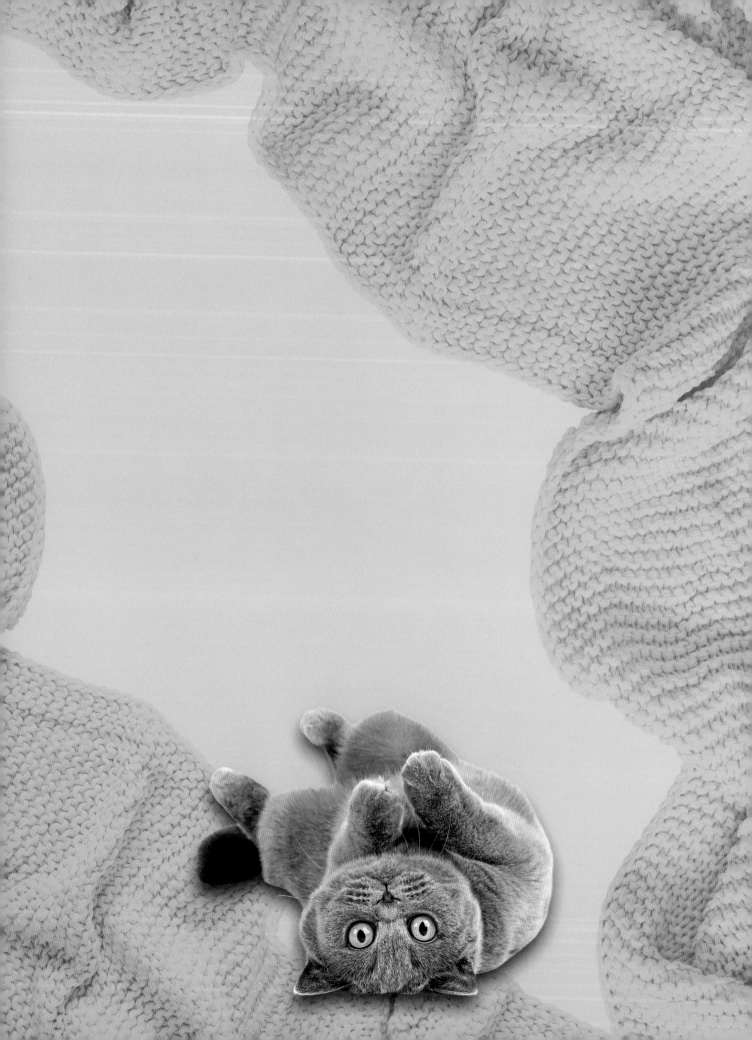

NATIONAL GEOGRAPHIC KiDS

CAN'T GET ENOUGH
Cat Stuff

FUN FACTS,
AWESOME
INFO, COOL
GAMES,
SILLY JOKES,
AND MORE!

MARA GRUNBAUM AND
BERNARD MENSAH

NATIONAL GEOGRAPHIC
WASHINGTON, D.C.

TABLE OF CONTENTS

CALLING ALL CAT LOVERS!

MEOW! Cats are popular pets all over the world. They cuddle on laps, pounce and prance after toys, leap like acrobats, and sometimes baffle us with their mysterious behavior. Cats come in a wide variety of colors and all kinds of coats, ranging from fluffy fur babies to bald beauties. Humans have had feline companions for thousands of years, whether they are our best buds or dependable mousers. It's no wonder we think they're the cat's pajamas!

This book is your ultimate source for cat fun. Inside, you'll find plenty of feline facts, such as why cats can see so well in the dark and which breeds are the fastest. Uncover the mysteries behind feline behavior through interviews with experts, and dig into quizzes to test your kitty cleverness. Plus, enjoy laugh-out-loud feline jokes, cat crafts, and awesome activities like word scrambles and matching games. Not sure how to pronounce a breed name? Check out the pronunciation guide on pages 122–123. Can't get enough of cats? Purrfect—just turn the page!

MANY EXPERTS RECOMMEND KEEPING CATS INDOORS FOR THEIR SAFETY, AND FOR THE SAFETY OF SMALL WILDLIFE.

IF YOU'D LIKE YOUR CAT TO ENJOY SOME OUTDOOR TIME, MAKE SURE TO RESEARCH PROPER SUPERVISION NEEDS AND SAFETY GEAR.

KITTEN MATCHUP

Kittens often look very different from grown-up cats. Can you match the kittens below to the adult cats of the same breed? On a sheet of paper, write the numbers 1–6. Next to each number, write the letter of the adult cat that you think that kitten will grow into. Compare your answers to the answer key at the bottom of page 9.

2

1

ADULT CATS

A

MAINE COON CAT

B

BENGAL

C

PERSIAN

3

5

4

6

D

SPHYNX

E

RAGDOLL

F

SIAMESE

THAT'S HISSTERICAL!

Q What's a cat's favorite activity at the fair?

A The pounce house.

Q Why are cats afraid of trees?

A Because of their bark.

Q What do you call a cat police officer?

A Claw enforcement.

Q How is a cat like a coin?

A Each has a head on one side and a tail on the other.

YOU'VE CAT TO BE KITTEN ME ...

Q What is the difference between a cat and a comma?

A One has the paws before the claws and the other has the clause before the pause.

Q What is a cat's favorite movie?

A The Sound of Mewsic.

Q What's another name for a cat's house?

A A scratch pad.

Q Why aren't cats great storytellers?

A They only have one tail to tell.

THE NITTY GRITTY OF KITTIES

Cats' wild relatives are built to stalk and kill prey. House cats may not be wild hunters, but they have the same basic body parts that wild cats have. Check out this diagram to learn all about a cat's furtastic features.

Eyes
Cats see well in dim light and have excellent peripheral vision—meaning they can detect movement much farther around the sides of their heads than humans can. Cats also have extra inner eyelids, called nictitating membranes. These act like windshield wipers to clean and moisten the eyes when cats blink.

Scent spreaders (cheek area)
Scent is an important way for cats to communicate. When they rub their heads against an object, body parts called glands on their foreheads, cheeks, and chin release a small amount of their scent. Cats use this chemical signal to mark their territory. Nuzzling you with their heads is a compliment—it means they're claiming you as their own!

Paws
"Toe beans" is the nickname for the squishy, jelly bean-shaped pads on the bottom of a cat's paws. Most cats have four toe beans (the technical term is digital pads) on each foot. These toe beans are where cats sweat!

Claws
A cat uses its curved claws for climbing, digging, fighting off attackers, and snagging prey. Cats usually have a claw on each toe and also have a claw farther up each leg, called the dewclaw. A cat can retract its claws when not using them to keep the claws from snagging or becoming dull.

Ears
Hearing is one of a cat's sharpest senses. Cat ears are especially good at picking up high-pitched noises, like those made by a bird or mouse. Thirty-two muscles in each ear allow a cat to swivel them in the direction a sound is coming from. Fluffy ear hair, also called "ear furnishings," helps keep debris out of these important organs.

Whiskers
Cats have stiff bristles called whiskers above their eyes, on the chin, and near the ears. These whiskers, or vibrissae, help cats figure out if they can fit into small spaces or openings. Each whisker is connected to nerve endings that respond to even the slightest movement. This helps a cat sense subtle vibrations and feel what's going on around it—almost like having fingers on your face!

Tail
A cat's tail is an extension of its spinal column. It contains up to 23 bones surrounded by muscles that help it bend and flex every which way. Cats use their tails for balance and to express how they're feeling.

Spinal column
A cat's vertebrae, or backbones, are connected by muscles, rather than stiffer connections called ligaments like humans have. This makes its spine extremely flexible—and allows a cat to do full-body twists while in the air to make sure it lands on its feet!

Shoulder blades
A cat's shoulder blades are connected to the rest of its body only by muscles—not by other bones. This allows cats to rotate their front legs in almost any direction and turn on a dime.

Skin and coat
Cats have "compound" hair follicles. This means that up to 15 hairs can grow out of a single pore. If a cat is scared, tiny muscles attached to each follicle cause the hair to bristle, or puff up, making the cat look bigger. Cats shed and regrow layers of their coats to keep their bodies at the temperature most comfortable for them.

Carpal whiskers (whiskers on backs of front legs)
In addition to their famous face whiskers, cats have sensitive vibrissae, known as carpal whiskers, on the backs of their front legs.

CATS IN THE PAST

CATS HAVE BEEN SPECIAL TO HUMANS FOR THOUSANDS OF YEARS.

In some parts of the ancient world, such as in ancient Egypt, they were even worshipped as gods and goddesses. Because they were considered sacred, cats were dressed in fine jewelry on important occasions. When cats died, they were sometimes mummified and buried in their owners' tombs. Ancient Egyptians also believed that the goddess Bastet could turn herself into a cat. Bastet was the goddess of protection from evil and bringer of good health. She was often depicted as a woman with the head of a cat. But ancient Egypt isn't the only culture that loved cats.

GOING GREEK

The ancient Greeks believed that Hecate, the goddess of witchcraft and magic, once transformed into a cat while trying to escape a giant monster named Typhon. After she escaped, she retained a fondness for felines, and the Greeks in turn treated cats with respect. In Greek society, cats eventually replaced snakes and weasels as household pets to get rid of rats and mice. And—like people today—ancient Greeks thought cats were funny! The playwright Aristophanes, for example, added cats to his plays for comedic effect.

JOURNEY TO JAPAN

People in ancient Japan also loved cats. Centuries ago, cats arrived in Japan by way of boats traveling to the country. They became popular domestic pets and even symbols of good luck. According to one Japanese legend, a cat sitting outside a temple once waved at a local ruler who was passing by. Intrigued by the waving cat, the ruler decided to enter the temple. After he stepped inside, lightning struck the spot where he had been standing. The cat had saved his life!

Today, maneki-neko, or lucky cat statues, are often seen throughout Japan and in movies and cartoons. Although statues may vary in size, shape, and color, most resemble the Japanese bobtail cat and have one raised paw. If the right paw is raised, it is said to attract money and good luck. If the left paw is raised, this supposedly attracts friendship—or customers, if it is at a shop. Which is your paw-ference?

SCIENTISTS THINK DOMESTICATED CATS DID NOT APPEAR IN THE AMERICAS UNTIL EUROPEAN EXPLORERS ARRIVED AROUND THE 1500s.

THE ANCIENT MAYA REVERED WILD CATS SUCH AS PANTHERS AND JAGUARS.

AN ARCHAEOLOGIST DISCOVERED CAT PAW PRINTS THAT WERE LEFT ON AN ANCIENT ROMAN ROOF TILE 2,000 YEARS AGO!

15

SMITTEN WITH KITTENS

CAN'T GET ENOUGH KITTENS? CHECK OUT THESE JUST-FOR-FUN FURRY RECORD HOLDERS!

BIGGEST LITTER

SIAMESE

The record for most kittens born in a litter goes to a Siamese—for 19 kittens! Siamese cats have been around since about the 14th century. They usually have four to six kittens per litter.

CURLIEST COAT

SELKIRK REX

The award for curliest coat goes to the Selkirk rex! Every hair on a Selkirk rex's body is curly, right down to the whiskers. As these kittens grow, their coat can go back and forth between extra curly to almost straight.

MOST PLAYFUL

ABYSSINIAN

Winning the award for most playful kitten is ... the Abyssinian! These spirited kittens often act like little clowns. The Abyssinian breed is known for being athletic and almost doglike in its desire to hang out with its human family. It's no wonder these cats are always ready to play!

EASIEST TO POTTY TRAIN

ALL KITTENS

Kittens definitely win the award for easiest animal for a human to potty train. They pick up on it faster than puppies—or human kids! Kittens learn to use the litter box by copying their mothers, so most kittens will already be litter-trained by the time they come home with you!

SOFTEST KITTEN

RAGDOLL

Ragdoll kittens take the prize of being one of the softest breeds. These fluffy felines are perfect snuggle buddies—they are even named for their tendency to collapse happily into their owners' arms. But these sweet kitties don't just lie around all day waiting to be petted. Ragdolls like to play and have even been known to learn how to fetch toys.

HOME SWEET HOME

There are many different breeds, or types, of cats. The exact number depends on which organization is doing the counting. Each breed has its own typical look, body type, and even personality. Many breeds originated in a particular location and have now spread around the world. This map shows where seven breeds were first found.

Breed: Sphynx
Origin: Toronto, Canada
Description: Medium-size, with strikingly large ears and wrinkly, almost entirely hairless skin
Fun Facts: In 1966, a kitten was born in Toronto, Canada, with a rare but harmless condition that left her with practically no hair. She was bred with another naturally hairless cat to develop this unique and striking breed.

NORTH AMERICA

Toronto, CANADA

ATLANTIC OCEAN

BRAZIL

SOUTH AMERICA

PACIFIC OCEAN

Breed: Brazilian shorthair
Origin: Brazil
Description: Large, muscular, and playful, with short and silky fur
Fun Facts: Known for its large ears and glossy coat, this cat tends to have an eye coloring that corresponds with the color of its coat.

Breed: Egyptian mau
Origin: Egypt
Description: Elegant and athletic, with distinctive spots and a striped tail
Fun Facts: One of the oldest known breeds, these kitties are thought to be descendants of the sacred cats of ancient Egypt. Archaeologists have found similar-looking cats depicted in art and mummified in royal tombs.

SOUTHERN OCEAN

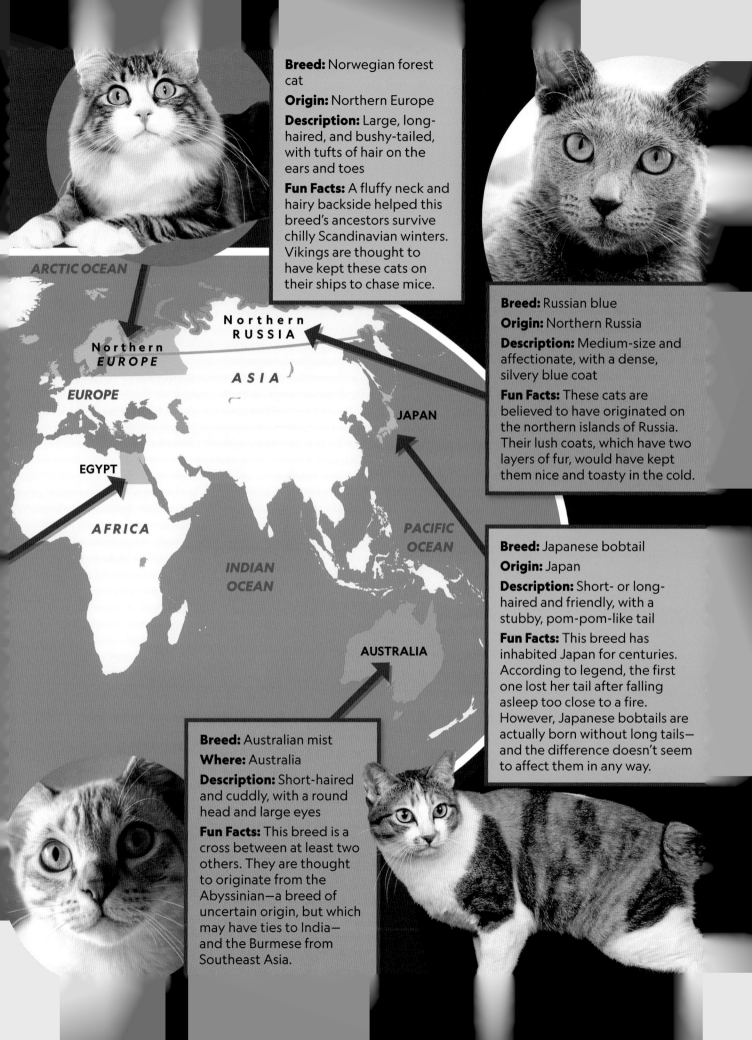

Breed: Norwegian forest cat

Origin: Northern Europe

Description: Large, long-haired, and bushy-tailed, with tufts of hair on the ears and toes

Fun Facts: A fluffy neck and hairy backside helped this breed's ancestors survive chilly Scandinavian winters. Vikings are thought to have kept these cats on their ships to chase mice.

Breed: Russian blue

Origin: Northern Russia

Description: Medium-size and affectionate, with a dense, silvery blue coat

Fun Facts: These cats are believed to have originated on the northern islands of Russia. Their lush coats, which have two layers of fur, would have kept them nice and toasty in the cold.

Breed: Japanese bobtail

Origin: Japan

Description: Short- or long-haired and friendly, with a stubby, pom-pom-like tail

Fun Facts: This breed has inhabited Japan for centuries. According to legend, the first one lost her tail after falling asleep too close to a fire. However, Japanese bobtails are actually born without long tails—and the difference doesn't seem to affect them in any way.

Breed: Australian mist

Where: Australia

Description: Short-haired and cuddly, with a round head and large eyes

Fun Facts: This breed is a cross between at least two others. They are thought to originate from the Abyssinian—a breed of uncertain origin, but which may have ties to India—and the Burmese from Southeast Asia.

ARCTIC OCEAN

Northern RUSSIA

Northern EUROPE

ASIA

EUROPE

JAPAN

EGYPT

AFRICA

PACIFIC OCEAN

INDIAN OCEAN

AUSTRALIA

LOTS OF CATTITUDE

CATS ARE CREPUSCULAR—MEANING THEY ARE MOST ACTIVE AT **dawn and dusk.**

According to scientists, cats **slow-blink** or narrow their eyes to show trust.

A CAT MAY REVEAL ITS BELLY WHEN IT FEELS COMFORTABLE AROUND YOU. BUT NO BELLY RUBS, PLEASE! CATS HAVE A NATURAL INSTINCT TO PROTECT THEIR STOMACHS.

Cats that are friends will sometimes **groom each other.**

DID YOU KNOW THAT MAMA CATS WILL OFTEN ADOPT ORPHAN KITTENS? FEMALE CATS HAVE A STRONG MOTHERLY INSTINCT—**ESPECIALLY IF THEY ALREADY HAVE A LITTER**—AND MANY WILL TAKE IN NEW KITTENS WITHOUT HESITATION.

A kitten's needly claws are out at all times before **IT LEARNS TO RETRACT THEM** at about one month old.

Experts think that **cats bring prey to their owners** to treat them like family and show them how to hunt.

Catnip, an herb that contains a natural chemical called nepetalactone, is found in many cat toys. CATNIP WILL OFTEN MAKE CATS FEEL HAPPY, AFFECTIONATE, OR PLAYFUL.

WHICH CAT BREED IS MOST LIKE YOU?

IF THESE DESCRIPTIONS DON'T FIT YOU, THAT'S OK. THIS QUIZ IS JUST FOR FUN!

Many people assume all cats are the same—but different breeds often have different personalities. Take this quiz to find out which cat breed best matches your personality.

1. When you're at a party, you can be found _____.

   a. making friends with the cat of the house

   b. clowning around and cracking jokes

   c. organizing a round of karaoke

2. When you're in school, you prefer to _____.

   a. study with a good friend

   b. give presentations or performances—you love all eyes on you

   c. practice your debate skills

3. If your class were to do a fashion show, what type of outfit would you choose?

   a. casual—your regular clothes will do just fine

   b. shiny and glittery—the more sparkle, the better

   c. elegant and stylish—nothing but the best

4. When you are at the pool, you like to _____.

   a. hang out at the shallow end with your friends

   b. swim laps for days

   c. do cannonballs and tricks

5. Which car would you most like to ride in?

   a. monster truck

   b. superfast sports car

   c. car equipped with all the latest technology

6. **What's your favorite type of TV show?**

   a. anything you can watch with the rest of the family

   b. comedy—you love a good laugh

   c. anything that explains how things work

CHECK YOUR SCORE.
Count up how many of each letter you have chosen. Then read the results below. If you have a tie score, read the results for both letters:

If you picked mostly a's: You are most like an American bobtail.
American bobtails are known for being loyal, loving, and extremely intelligent. They adore spending time with people and getting to know them. These cats also love to show off their wild instincts, sometimes even catching insects midair!

If you picked mostly b's: You are most like a Bengal.
These cats are full of energy and can even be a little bit mischievous! They are also one of the few breeds that love water and will dive straight in. Bengals are loud and opinionated and will let you know when they want something and exactly what it is.

If you picked mostly c's: You are most like a Siamese.
Siamese cats are very intelligent—many owners have even reported they can twist knobs to open doors! These kitties are known to be social and outgoing, but they also love a relaxing snuggle session!

CAT COMEDY

Q What did the alien say to the cat?

A "Take me to your litter!"

Q How does one cat tell another cat it's sorry?

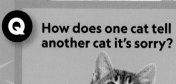

A "I apawlogize. I didn't mean to hurt your felines!"

Q Why do cats make the best DJs?

A They know how to scratch records!

TONGUE TWISTER

SAY THIS FAST THREE TIMES:

The curious cat climbed carefully across the crevices in the crawl space.

YOU'VE CAT TO BE KITTEN ME ...

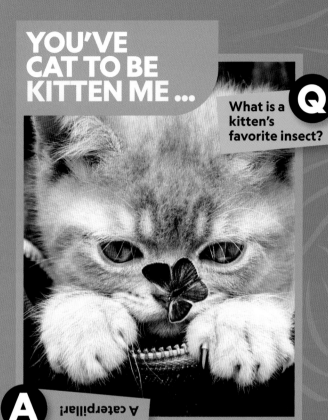

Q What is a kitten's favorite insect?

A A caterpillar!

SASHA: Have you heard the joke about the cat that went to the grocery store?

AYANA: Yeah, but I didn't find it amewsing.

Q What's a cat's favorite cooking tool?

A A whisker.

Q What do you get when you cross a cat with a parrot?

A A carrot.

KITTY CARETAKER

DR. YUKI HATTORI, VETERINARIAN

Dr. Yuki Hattori is a veterinarian. But unlike other vets, who often treat all types of pets, Dr. Hattori focuses on felines. He has written a book called *What Cats Want,* and he founded the Tokyo Feline Medical Center, where he sees more than 10,000 patients every year. Here, Dr. Hattori shares what it's like to be a cat-care specialist.

DID YOU ALWAYS WANT TO BE A CAT VETERINARIAN?

I decided to become a veterinarian when I was a teenager, but I thought I wanted to work with wild cats. I went to the zoo in my town many times to see lions, tigers, leopards, snow leopards, and other felines. In my fifth year of veterinary school, I met a family of domestic cats at a convenience store. The kittens were about 10 days old and just opening their eyes. After a while, the mother cat decided to move to a new location, and she took the kittens one by one. But she left one kitten behind. I was worried about that kitten, so I decided to take care of it. Living with this cat, Unya, made me fascinated with house cats. I decided then that I wanted to work to save cats' lives.

WHAT IS IT LIKE TO TREAT CATS FOR A LIVING?

It can be challenging to work with cats, because most of them don't like coming to the vet. They don't want to be poked and prodded and held by strangers in an unfamiliar place. Even if they're sick and they feel better afterward, they don't understand that going to the vet was the reason. I think it's cute when they're feisty and don't want to cooperate with us. But it can make it more difficult to get exams and procedures done.

HOW CAN CAT OWNERS HELP THEIR PETS STAY HEALTHY?

It can be hard for people to know when their cats are sick, because it isn't always obvious from the outside. Cats are good at hiding their discomfort, so a sick cat may appear to us to be perfectly healthy. Regular vet visits can help us detect and treat diseases sooner, though.

WHAT ADVICE DO YOU HAVE FOR CAT OWNERS?

People sometimes find their cats' behavior confusing. They'll say things like, "I was holding the cat and he seemed comfortable, but then he bit me out of nowhere!" Cats do give signs when they don't want to be held, though. Their ears might be pointed down, and their tails might be flicking back and forth. Many people don't notice these signals, but we can learn to understand them. Cats aren't always easy, and they don't always do what humans want. But I think that's their charm!

IF YOU HAVE A CAT, ASK YOUR VET FOR TIPS ON HOW TO MAKE YOUR CAT'S CHECKUPS LESS STRESSFUL!

DID YOU KNOW THAT A CAT'S SPINE IS

VERY FLEXIBLE?

BECAUSE OF THIS FLEXIBILITY, CATS CAN ARCH THEIR BACKS INTO AN

UPSIDE-DOWN U SHAPE.

WHEN A

CAT

IS FALLING,

ITS FLEXIBLE BACK CAN TWIST IN MIDAIR
AND HELP IT LAND UPRIGHT.

CATS CAN (ALMOST ALWAYS) LAND ON THEIR FEET. THIS IS PARTLY THANKS TO THE VESTIBULAR SYSTEM. THE VESTIBULAR SYSTEM IS MADE OF SEVERAL BODY PARTS THAT TOGETHER LET A CAT KNOW WHICH WAY IS UP. MANY OTHER ANIMALS HAVE A VESTIBULAR SYSTEM, TOO—INCLUDING HUMANS!

NEVER PURPOSELY DROP A CAT FROM ANY HEIGHT. IT CAN STILL GET HURT!

FURRY FAMILY

Cats are members of the feline family. Their relatives include tigers, leopards, and more than 30 other species. Take a look at how an average house cat compares in size to other felines. (Then imagine if a lion were trying to curl up on the couch!)

Mountain lion
Puma concolor
WEIGHT: up to 175 pounds (80 kg)
That's 17.5 times as big as a house cat.

Domestic cat
Felis catus
AVERAGE WEIGHT:
10 pounds (4.5 kg)

European wildcat
Felis silvestris
WEIGHT: up to 13 pounds (6 kg)
That's about the same size as a very large domestic cat.

Snow leopard
Panthera uncia
WEIGHT: up to 120 pounds (55 kg)
That's 12 times as big as a house cat.

African lion
Panthera leo
WEIGHT: up to 550 pounds (250 kg)

That's 55 times as big as a house cat.

Tiger
Panthera tigris
WEIGHT: up to 496 pounds (225 kg)

That's 50 times as big as a house cat!

A TALL TAIL

By the time they are **six weeks old**, kittens are already using their tails for balance as they **walk, pounce, and play.**

The nerves in a cat's tail communicate directly with its brain, which helps it stay upright while jumping, falling, or twisting.

CATS USE THEIR TAILS TO BALANCE WHEN CLIMBING OR WALKING ON NARROW SURFACES.

AN ARCHED BACK AND PUFFY TAIL might be a sign that a cat is UPSET. A cat's bushy tail makes it seem larger, which can help scare off predators.

CATS MIGHT SLOWLY **SWAY THEIR TAILS BACK AND FORTH** WHEN THEY ARE FEELING PLAYFUL.

While the length of a cat's tail depends on the breed, the standard tail lengths are 9.9 inches (25.1 cm) for female cats and 11 inches (27.9 cm) for male cats.

When a cat is asleep, a moving tail may be a sign the cat is dreaming.

An alert cat whipping its tail back and forth is likely nervous or ANGRY.

Turn the page for more facts about cat tails!

Cats use their tails to communicate with other cats, and with humans.

Some cats use their tails to give **"hugs"** by twining them with another cat's tail, or even by wrapping their tails around your leg!

Domestic cats are the only felines that hold their tails **straight up while walking.**

A cat has around 18 to 23 vertebrae **in its tail alone.** That's more than half the amount in **a human's entire spine!**

SOME SCIENTISTS HAVE ANALYZED WHICH PARTS OF A CAT'S BODY ARE **THE BEST FOR PETTING—** and the answer doesn't include the tail. Because a cat's tail is very sensitive, MOST CATS PREFER TO BE PETTED ON THE BACK OF THEIR HEADS OR UNDER THEIR CHINS.

A cat with a floppy tail should be brought to the vet right away—IT COULD BE A SIGN THAT THE CAT IS SICK OR INJURED.

A cat that's holding its tail **straight with a curve at the tip** is likely saying hello.

TONGUE TWISTERS

If a cat has ever licked you, you may have noticed something surprising. Instead of feeling smooth or slippery, a cat's tongue can feel like sandpaper on your skin. That's because it's covered in hundreds of tiny curved spines, which scientists call papillae. These unique structures act like a built-in comb to help cats detangle their fur while they groom.

POWER WASH

Technology has helped scientists unravel the secrets of how cats' tongues help them clean themselves. In 2018, engineers at the Georgia Institute of Technology examined cat tongues using slow-motion video and powerful microscopes. They found that the papillae, which normally point back toward a cat's mouth, can rotate as they press into the fur. This helps the cat untangle knots and reach the deepest layers of its coat with each lick. Close-up scans revealed that the tip of each tongue spine is actually hollow. These cavities wick saliva from the cat's mouth onto its body as it grooms. The small amount of spit helps the cat achieve a deeper clean than it would otherwise. Over the course of a day, a cat transfers about one fifth of a cup (47mL) of liquid onto its hair and skin!

DRINK UP!

Cleaning themselves isn't the only thing cats' tongues are good for. Kitties also have a clever way of using their tongues to drink. Researchers at the Massachusetts Institute of Technology took slow-motion video of cats lapping up liquid, then analyzed the footage. They were surprised to find that cats use their tongues very differently from how dogs do.

Dogs drink by sticking out their tongues and shaping them into big scoops. They use these scoops to pick up water and slosh it into their mouths. Cats, on the other hand, curl their tongues into a J shape and touch only the tip to the water's surface. As a cat pulls its tongue back in, some of the water follows it, forming a column of liquid. The cat snaps its mouth shut just in time to catch the water before gravity pulls it back into the bowl. This efficient strategy makes cats much tidier drinkers than dogs.

IF A CAT LICKS YOU, IT MIGHT BE A SIGN OF TRUST. CATS GROOM EACH OTHER TO SHOW AFFECTION, AND "GROOMING" HUMANS CAN MEAN THE SAME THING.

HOUSE CATS LAP WATER ABOUT FOUR TIMES PER SECOND. THEIR LARGER RELATIVES, INCLUDING LIONS, LAP MORE SLOWLY BECAUSE THEY HAVE BIGGER TONGUES.

THAT'S HISSTERICAL!

Q What's it called when all the treats are gone?

A A catastrophe!

Q Where do cats go on a field trip?

A The mewseum.

Q What did the cat say when it fell off the table?

A "Me-OW!"

YOU'VE CAT TO BE KITTEN ME ...

Q Which side of a cat has the most fur?

A The outside.

KNOCK, KNOCK.

Who's there?
Hans.
Hans who?
Hans off my tuna!

TASTE TEST

It's 6 a.m. and Fluffy is sitting on your head. She's saying it's time for breakfast, whether you like it or not. If you are going to get up, you might as well fill her bowl with food she really likes! Conduct a taste test to see which kibble deserves a nibble.

YOU WILL NEED:
BLUE PAINTER'S TAPE
YARDSTICK OR METERSTICK
9 SMALL PAPER PLATES
2 TYPES OF DRY CAT FOOD
PLAIN DRIED CRANBERRIES
PENCIL AND PAPER

THE FOODS LISTED HERE ARE SAFE FOR MOST CATS TO EAT IN MODERATION. HOWEVER, MAKE SURE TO CHECK WITH AN EXPERT BEFORE FEEDING YOUR CAT NEW THINGS.

STEP 1:
Prepare the grid. In a clear area of the floor, use painter's tape to create a square one yard by one yard (1 m by 1 m) wide. Use more tape to divide the square into nine equal boxes, each about one foot (30 cm) wide.

STEP 2:
Count three pieces of each type of food and three dried cranberries. Place one piece on a plate in each square on your grid. Mix it up—don't put all of the same kinds of food next to each other.

STEP 3:

Draw the grid on your piece of paper and write down what you put in each square.

STEP 4:

Just before mealtime, when your cat is hungry, place her in front of the grid. Use your paper to record the order in which she eats the food selections.

STEP 5:

Review the list. Did your cat choose one food over the others? Were there any foods your cat wouldn't eat at all?

TRYING NEW FOODS CAN BE FUN! BUT YOU SHOULD NEVER FORCE YOUR CAT OR CATS TO DO SOMETHING THEY DON'T WANT TO DO.

CONCLUSION:

Cats may taste a tiny bit of new food and wait to see how they feel. Most cats will slowly adjust to a new diet if they are fed the new food often. On the other hand, if your kitty scarfed down both cat foods and the dried cranberries, you're not dealing with a picky eater. They will be happy with any nutritional food you put in their bowl!

WHEN A CAT WANTS TO

MARK ITS TERRITORY,

IT HAS A FEW DIFFERENT OPTIONS:

SCRATCHING

SOMETHING,

RUBBING

ITS FACE AGAINST IT, OR

PEEING

ON IT.

EACH OF THESE ACTIONS LEAVES BEHIND THE CAT'S SCENT.

CATS COMMUNICATE THROUGH SCENT. A CAT'S SCENT LETS OTHER CATS KNOW TO STAY AWAY— THIS TERRITORY IS CLAIMED!

FROM WILDCAT TO HOUSE CAT

PEOPLE MAY CALL DOGS "MAN'S BEST FRIEND," BUT CATS HAVE ALSO KEPT HUMANS COMPANY FOR THOUSANDS OF YEARS. So, where exactly did the modern house cat come from? And how did we end up with so many breeds? Dive in and find out!

ANCIENT ORIGINS

It's hard for scientists and archaeologists to track exactly who had the first domestic cat—partly because the skeletons of wild cats and domestic cats are very similar. But certain archaeological discoveries, such as cat bones found near ancient human settlements, show that domestic cats have been around people for at least 12,000 years.

Scientists believe that cats were first domesticated in the Near East and are descendants of the Middle Eastern wildcat *Felis silvestris*. When humans started growing crops and storing grain, they soon realized that cats could catch mice and keep the grain safe. Over the centuries, people began to keep kitties not just as loyal mousers, but also as companions and friends. Some people were even buried with their cats.

VERY SUPERSTITIOUS

Cats have been around for thousands of years and are beloved to this day, but they weren't always such popular pets. Felines did appear favorably as sacred creatures in both Egyptian and Greek mythology, but black cats in medieval Europe became closely tied to witches and witchcraft. These stories and rumors gave them a bad reputation. Many people even thought they acted as servants for witches or other creepy creatures.

But it's not all bad news! While some people struggled with superstitions toward cats, others believed they brought good luck. For example, in Japan, a cat crossing your path meant good fortune was on its way. Even some parts of Europe warmed to the black cat; in the Midlands in England, black cats were considered the ideal lucky wedding present for a bride. And in Italy, people believed that even hearing a black cat sneeze would bring about a streak of good luck.

THE MODERN HOUSE CAT

Thankfully, cats don't carry a bad reputation anymore. In fact, felines are downright beloved. From cat videos on the internet to cartoon cats like Garfield, humans have embraced their feline friends. Many people even began to purposely breed them, creating different cat breeds with a range of different personalities. Today, there are 45 breeds recognized internationally by the Cat Fanciers' Association. From the Abyssinian to the Turkish Van, cats have stolen our hearts and made a comfy place for themselves in our homes.

CAT COMEDY

KNOCK, KNOCK.

Who's there?
Tabby.
Tabby who?
I'd like tabby let in now, please!

Q What is a cat's favorite color?

A Purple.

Q Why don't domestic cats invite wild cats to their board game nights?

A Because some wild cats are cheetahs!

LAUGHABLE LIST

A cat's top jobs

Mousekeeper
....
Anthropawlogist
....
Furniture maker
....
Meowgician

VETERINARIAN 1: This Maine coon cat has the biggest feet I've ever seen!

VETERINARIAN 2: Wow, are you sure?

VETERINARIAN 1: I'm pawsitive!

YOU'VE CAT TO BE KITTEN ME ...

Q What is a cat's favorite treat?

A Mice cream.

TOP TAILS

Cat tails come in all varieties, from fluffy to sleek ... to no tail at all! Check out these just-for-fun records for some of the most awesome cat tails around.

SHORTEST TAIL

MANX

The Manx from the Isle of Man wins the award for shortest tail. Some Manx are born with small stubs, while others are born with no tails at all. But short tails or no tails, these cats are famed for their hunting skills.

FLUFFIEST TAIL

SOMALI

It's hard to resist the fluffiness of a Somali's tail. These cats often have bushy red fur and foxlike tails that require quite a bit of grooming. Somalis are also very athletic and often have a love of climbing.

LONGEST TAIL

MAINE COON CAT

Maine coon cats are known for their long fluffy fur and their even longer tails. In fact, the world record holder for longest tail belongs to a Maine coon cat! Their bushy tails can grow to almost 18 inches (46 cm) long. This isn't surprising though, as Maine coon cats are among the largest domesticated cat breeds.

BALDEST TAIL

SPHYNX

The best known of all the hairless cat breeds, the sphynx isn't actually completely bald; most have a thin fuzz covering their bodies, with more hair on their heads, tails, and paws. The skin of a sphynx is also very loose, which contributes to its wrinkly look.

CURLIEST TAIL

JAPANESE BOBTAILS

Did you know that some cats—like some Japanese bobtails—have permanently curled tails? Japanese bobtails are known to be very social cats that love spending time with humans—and with other Japanese bobtails!

BREED BONANZA

There are so many types of cats in the world—can you unscramble the letters to find the names of eight different cat breeds? Give it a try!

1. KRIKSEL XER

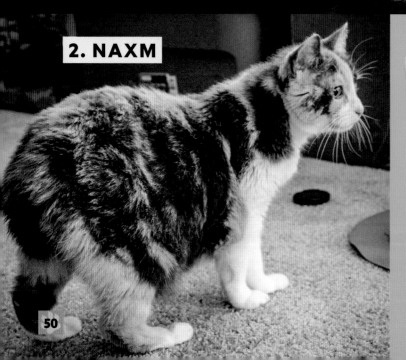

2. NAXM

3. NASTARUAIL SITM

Answer Key: 1. Selkirk rex; 2. Manx; 3. Australian mist; 4. Somali; 5. Ragdoll; 6. Abyssinian; 7. Bengal; 8. Scottish fold

4. MOAISL

6. YNSBSIANIA

7. GENBAL

8. HITTSCOS DOLF

5. DALLGRO

CAT CULTURE

Different languages use different words for the noise a cat makes. In English, **"meow"** is often used. Some other words are:

miaou (French),
miau (Spanish),
yaong (Korean),
nyan (Japanese), and
miyav (Turkish).

A GROUP OF KITTENS is sometimes called a **kindle**. A group of adult cats is called a **clowder**.

AUGUST 8 IS INTERNATIONAL CAT DAY!

The first official cat show was held in 1871 in London, England, at the grand Crystal Palace. It included a huge exhibit of cat breeds from all over the world.

A RESCUE KITTY NAMED NALA HOLDS THE WORLD RECORD FOR **MOST FOLLOWED CAT ON INSTAGRAM** AFTER WINNING THE HEARTS OF MORE THAN 4.5 MILLION FOLLOWERS.

HAVE YOU EVER WANTED TO TAKE YOUR CAT OUT AND ABOUT WITH YOU? WELL, THERE ARE **SPECIAL CAT BACKPACKS** MADE FOR THAT EXACT PURPOSE. THESE SPACIOUS BACKPACKS GIVE CATS PLACES TO SIT AND EVEN HAVE LITTLE WINDOWS FOR PEERING OUT.

In England, domestic cats are often called **moggies.**

Did you know that the United States is the country with the most domestic cats, AT MORE THAN 76 MILLION?

One cat inherited **seven million British pounds** (or 12.5 million U.S. dollars) when his antiques dealer owner passed away in 1988. That was one rich cat!

MAINE COON CATS

ARE AMONG THE

HEAVIEST BREEDS

OF DOMESTIC CAT.

THE AVERAGE MALE

WEIGHS IN SOMEWHERE BETWEEN

18 AND 25 POUNDS
(8–11 KG),

ALTHOUGH SOME HAVE BEEN

KNOWN TO REACH
30 POUNDS (14 KG).

THE SINGAPURA IS THE SMALLEST BREED IN THE WORLD; ON AVERAGE, EACH WEIGHS JUST FOUR POUNDS (2 KG).

FELINE QUIZ

Sharpen your feline fascination with this quiz! Write your answers on a piece of paper and check the answer key below when you've finished. Having trouble deciding on an answer? Try reading through the first half of the book again for a little help.

1. **Which ancient cultures adored cats?**
   a. Egyptian
   b. Greek
   c. Japanese
   d. all of the above

2. **Which of these breeds has the curliest fur?**
   a. Sphynx
   b. Singapura
   c. Manx
   d. Selkirk rex

3. **How many times per second do house cats lap water?**
   a. 2 times per second
   b. 4 times per second
   c. 8–10 times per second
   d. Zero. They like to sip their water.

4. **Why are cats so flexible?**
   a. They have an amazing yoga teacher.
   b. They practice martial arts from the time they are kittens.
   c. Their vertebrae are held together by muscles rather than ligaments.
   d. They have very few bones.

5. **What are ear furnishings?**
   a. a perfect set of ear-warmers for cold weather
   b. special furniture made of ears
   c. long hair inside a cat's ears
   d. a new and improved set of headphones

6. Which of these cat breeds is characterized by long hair and prominent ear tufts?

    a. Norwegian forest cat

    b. Bombay

    c. Sphynx

    d. Siamese

7. What is another word for a group of cats?

    a. herd

    b. feline flock

    c. mew crew

    d. clowder

8. True or False? Cats are messier drinkers than dogs.

9. If you love fluffy tails, what cat breed might be the best for you?

    a. Somali

    b. Egyptian mau

    c. American shorthair

    d. Bengal

10. True or False? Cats may expose their belly when they are nervous or feel threatened.

Answer Key: 1. d; 2. d; 3. b; 4. c; 5. c; 6. a; 7. d; 8. False. Cats pull up a column of water with the tip of their tongues, then quickly catch it in their mouths. This makes them less messy than dogs! 9. a; 10. False. Cats have an instinct to protect their stomachs, and usually don't expose their bellies unless they feel safe and comfortable.

SPEEDY CATS

While cats generally love to sleep and lounge in the sun, these particular felines are also known for their speed—or lack of it! Check out these just-for-fun records.

SPEEDY HUNTERS

CHARTREUX

Historians think these excellent hunters may have originally been brought to France from Syria around the Middle Ages and bred for their mousing skills. Chartreux cats are also known for their soft gray coats, bright coppery eyes, and loving personalities.

FASTEST DOMESTIC CAT

EGYPTIAN MAU

The Egyptian mau can sprint up to 30 miles an hour (48 km/h)! For reference, the world record for fastest human sprint is only 27 miles an hour (43 km/h).

SLOWEST CAT

PERSIAN

OK, so they can certainly sprint when they want to—but these friendly cats prefer to just lounge around.

CAT REFLEXES

ALL CATS

From twisting in midair to landing on their feet to swiping up prey, cats have incredible reflexes that are fantastically fast. In fact, a cat's reflexes are about 1.5 times faster than a dog's!

FAST SWIMMER

TURKISH VAN

Turkish Vans are one of the few cat breeds that love water. In fact, some people even refer to the breed as "the swimming cats." When not swimming or playing in water, these cats are often getting their energy out by chasing toys or jumping to high places.

NO PLACE LIKE HOME

Owners should have at least one litter box per cat, plus one extra. Felines prefer privacy, and some will not use the same litter box another cat has just used.

The best way to make sure your cat is comfortable in a carrier is to let your cat explore it beforehand. That way, your cat is familiar with the carrier come travel day.

Adopt me!

In the U.S., about **2.1 million cats** are adopted from shelters to find their furever homes each year.

CATS CAN LIVE IN A VARIETY OF ENVIRONMENTS, FROM ICY MOUNTAINS TO STEAMY, TROPICAL JUNGLES. **ANTARCTICA** IS THE ONLY CONTINENT WITH CONDITIONS THAT ARE **TOO HARSH** FOR DOMESTIC CATS TO SURVIVE OUTSIDE.

Cats knead when they feel safe and **content** in their environment. This is a soothing behavior **KITTENS LEARN WHEN THEY ARE NURSING.**

DOMESTIC CATS don't usually **MARK THEIR TERRITORY** by spraying their urine—but **WILD CATS DO!**

CATS LOVE TO CLIMB. IT PROVIDES GOOD EXERCISE AND A SAFE PLACE FOR A CAT TO SURVEY ITS TERRITORY.

DIY FEATHER TOY

What's that? A bird? A new sock to destroy? No, it's the fantastic feather flier! Playful kitties like fluffy feathers and toys that move. Put the two together with this feather flier.

YOU WILL NEED:
YARN OR STRING
PLASTIC CLOTHES HANGER
TAPE
CRAFT FEATHERS
SAFETY SCISSORS
SMALL BINDER CLIPS OR CLOTHESPINS

STEP 1:
Cut four pieces of yarn or string, each nine to 12 inches (23 to 30 cm) long.

STEP 2:
Tie the strings at equal distances across the bar of the hanger. Tape the knots in place so they do not slide around when your kitty plays with the toy.

DON'T HAVE A CAT? CONSIDER DONATING YOUR FEATHER TOY TO A LOCAL ANIMAL SHELTER OR RESCUE ORGANIZATION.

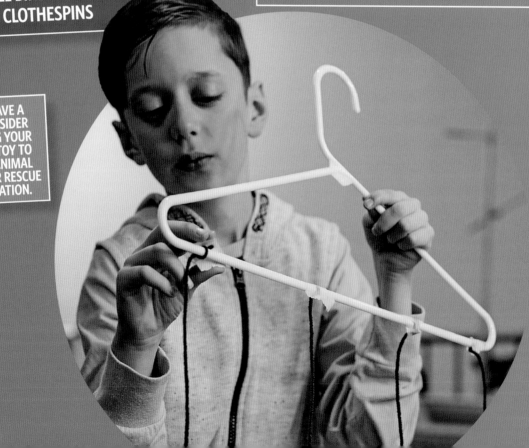

STEP 3:

Tie the other end of each piece of string to a binder clip or clothespin. Tape the knots to secure them. Clip a feather to each one.

SAFETY FIRST! MONITOR YOUR CAT WHILE PLAYING WITH THIS TOY. SMALL PIECES MAY FALL OFF AND HARM YOUR CAT IF INGESTED.

STEP 4:

Hang the hanger on the edge of a table or a doorknob and give it a little push to make the feathers fly.

TAKE IT FURTHER:

Swap out the feathers with other fluffy or wiggly things, like ribbons, felt, or pipe cleaners. Which does your cat like best?

THAT'S HISSTERICAL!

Q

What do cats wear to sleep?

A

Pawjamas!

Q

When is it bad luck to see a black cat?

A

When you are a mouse.

Q

What do you call a cat that loves bowling?

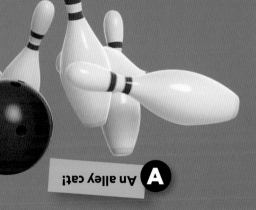

A

An alley cat!

Q Why should you never give a cat the TV remote?

A Because she will keep pawsing the show.

Q What's smarter than a talking cat?

A A spelling bee!

Q What has a head like a cat, feet like a cat, a tail like a cat, but isn't a cat?

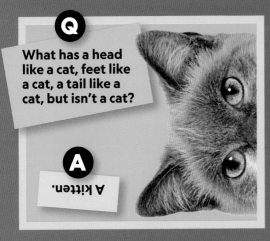

A A kitten.

Q Where's a cat's favorite vacation spot?

A The Canary Islands!

Q Why do cats enjoy sitting on computers?

A They like to keep an eye on the mouse.

MASTERS OF STEALTH

They may spend most of their time napping on couches these days, but house cats are born hunters. Their wild ancestors kept themselves alive by catching and killing animals such as small rodents, lizards, and birds. These prey animals can move quickly and are always on the lookout for predators. This means cats need to be sneaky if they want to snag a meal. Many parts of a cat's body work together to help it stalk and catch prey while remaining undetected. Scientists are still learning more about what gives kitties their killer moves.

ON THE PROWL

When a cat is stalking prey, it moves slowly, with its leg muscles flexed and its body in a crouched position. This helps it avoid being spotted by the prey that is about to become its dinner. Scientists at Duke University in North Carolina, U.S.A., have found that cats use a lot more energy moving this way than walking normally. But the trade-off is worth it: Their chance of a successful hunt is greatly increased.

A cat usually hears or smells its prey before it sees it. But once it has identified a potential victim, the cat locks eyes on the target, too. Felines use all their senses to track their prey's movements as they approach. Padded paws help a kitty creep closer slowly and silently until it's in good range to pounce.

READY, AIM, POUNCE!

No matter how stealthily a cat approaches its prey, it often has only one chance to grab it. As soon as the cat makes its move, its prey will notice—and possibly escape. So, cats take their time watching and waiting for exactly the right moment. They often wiggle their butts slightly before pouncing, which scientists think might help to warm up their muscles or line up a more precise strike.

When a cat springs into action, many muscles work together. Most adult cats can jump more than five feet (1.5 m)—several times their body length! But a cat's eyes can't focus on anything closer than one foot (30 cm) from its face, so another sense takes over. Researchers have used slow-motion video to show that a cat's whiskers snap forward in the final moments of an attack. As the cat's face gets closer to the prey, the sensitive whiskers make the first contact. They tell the cat where the prey is in relation to its mouth so it can go in for the killer bite.

Nowadays, many cats live indoors and don't have to hunt live animals. But they love to indulge their predator instincts by stalking, pouncing on, and biting their favorite toys. Experts agree that it's important to provide cats with lots of opportunities for this kind of playtime. Not only is it good exercise, it also keeps them connected to their wild roots.

SOME CATS LIKE TO POUNCE AT THINGS MOVING ON A TV SCREEN OR ON THE SCREENS OF OTHER DEVICES.

HAIR BALL!

HUUUURRRRKK! REEEE-UCK! GRRRR-AAAACK!

These are just some of the awkward sounds you might hear if a cat near you is hacking up a hair ball. This dramatic display is fairly common for cats, and it's typically harmless. As gross as it might seem, it's an important part of keeping a kitty's digestive system running as it should.

BALLING UP

Grooming is one of a cat's most important daily activities. Cats spend up to half of their waking hours licking themselves to remove dirt, debris, oils, and loose hairs. But cats have no choice but to swallow whatever they pick up with their spiny tongues. Swallowed hair collects in the stomach, where it can't be broken down.

Most of this hair gradually makes its way into the intestines. It travels alongside digested food and eventually gets pooped into the litter box. But some hair can form clumps that get stuck in the stomach. Cats need another way to remove it, which is where the upchucking comes in.

EXCUSE YOU!

To prepare to cough up a hair ball, a cat first crouches down and extends its neck. This position straightens its esophagus—the tube that connects the mouth to the stomach—to create a clear path for the hair ball to exit. Then the cat's stomach contracts repeatedly, forcing the hairy mass up and out of the esophagus—and causing the alarming noises. The narrow esophagus squeezes the wet hair into a sausage shape before it comes out.

The scientific name for a hair ball is a trichobezoar (try saying that fast three times). It's common for cats to cough up one of the slimy globs every few weeks or so. Unfortunately, it's also common for them to do so on furniture or hard-to-clean rugs—and anywhere you might not notice until you step in something wet.

KITTENS AND YOUNG CATS GET FAR FEWER HAIR BALLS THAN OLDER CATS, WHO ARE MORE METICULOUS ABOUT CLEANING THEMSELVES.

BIG CATS CAN GET HAIR BALLS, TOO. IN 2015, VETERINARY SURGEONS REMOVED A FOUR-POUND (2-KG) MASS OF HAIR FROM THE BELLY OF AN AFRICAN LION NAMED ARTHUR.

ON THE JOB

IF THESE DESCRIPTIONS DON'T FIT YOU, THAT'S OK. THIS QUIZ IS JUST FOR FUN!

Take this quiz to find the cat-related job that's the best fit for you.

1. **How do you get ready in the morning?**
   a. I try on lots of creative outfits.
   b. I wake up immediately and then help my family get ready.
   c. I take a nice, long shower—I love being squeaky clean.

2. **It's just you, a blank piece of paper, and lots of colored pencils. You draw_____.**
   a. your favorite animal
   b. a maze for your friends to find their way out of
   c. cool gadgets

3. **Your room right now is mostly filled with _____.**
   a. art supplies—can't live without 'em
   b. pets—can't get enough of 'em
   c. books—gotta have 'em

4. **Your favorite class in school is _____.**
   a. art
   b. gym
   c. science

5. **You and your friends have discovered a deep, dark cave. You _____.**
   a. create an art piece inspired by what you see
   b. lead your friends in, carefully instructing them on what to do
   c. take lots of notes of your observations

7. Your locker at school is _____.

a. full of posters and photographs

b. full of how-to books on tons of subjects

c. super organized and carefully labeled

6. It's time to cook a new recipe. You prefer to _____.

a. wing it—as long as it tastes good, who cares

b. get a parent to teach you their favorite recipe

c. follow the instructions in a cookbook carefully

CHECK YOUR SCORE. Count up how many of each letter you have chosen. Then read the results below. If you have a tie score, read the results for both letters:

Mostly a's: Cat toy designer
Cat toy designers are true magicians. They spend a large part of their day thinking about cats and what makes them happy. It's also a challenging job because the designers need to think of new ways to excite cats or find ways to make existing toys better (and that involves some science, too). If you chose mostly a's, your creative abilities are top-notch. This means that your imagination is suited for this job, so what are you waiting for? Start designing!

Mostly b's: Cat trainer
Cat trainers are like superheroes. They swoop in to help answer any questions you may have about why your cat may be behaving a certain way, and they can give you tips and tricks to help make your relationship with your cat even better. On an average day, a cat trainer may visit several pets for training sessions. Many pets will have multiple sessions with a trainer, so you may get to see the same feline friends and get to know each of their unique personalities. If you answered mostly b's, your deep love of animals, skill at teaching others, and ability to follow instructions could make you a great cat trainer.

Mostly c's: Veterinarian
Vets are the superstars of the cat community. They make sure that cats get all the care they need to stay healthy. They do examinations and give advice to owners (and sometimes give pets a little treat if they behave!). Vets also perform surgeries on cats that don't feel well. They are all about making sure cats stay in tip-top condition. If your answers were mostly c's, then you're organized and may love science. Becoming a vet requires lots and lots of studying. You might just have everything it takes to help cats get better and stay healthy!

CAT COMEDY

KNOCK, KNOCK.

Who's there?
Scratch.
Scratch who?
Scratch that—I decided to stay outside after all.

Q What do you call a cat wrapped up in a blanket?

A A purrito!

Q Where do cats keep all their loose hair?

A In the shed!

TONGUE TWISTER

SAY THIS FAST THREE TIMES:

Four fierce feline friends frolic freely.

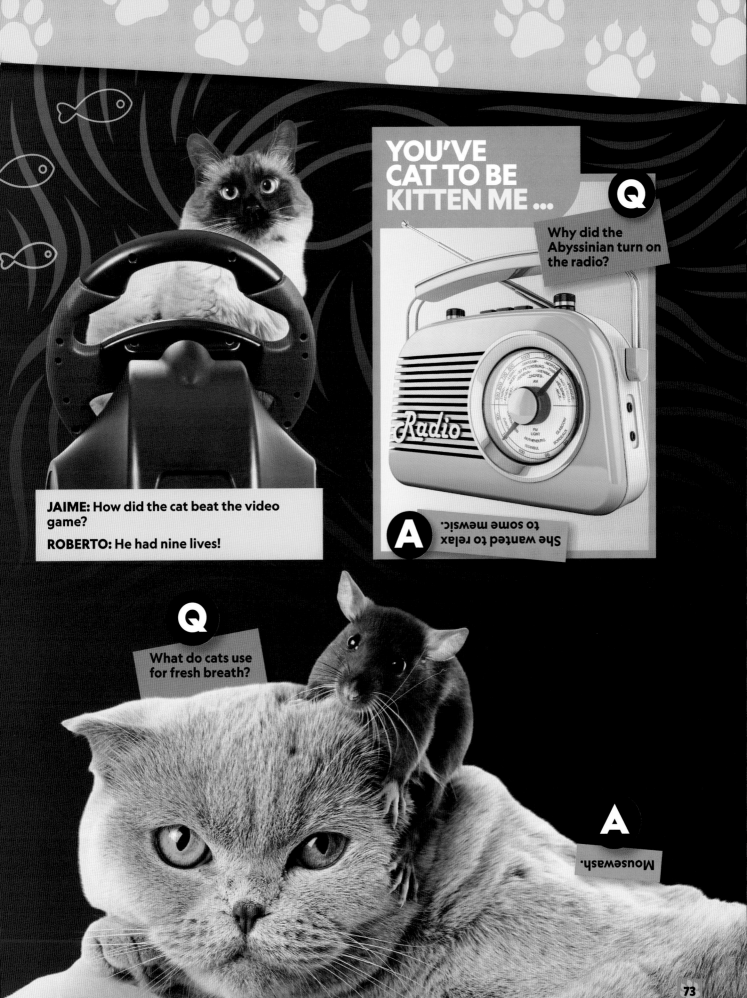

YOU'VE CAT TO BE KITTEN ME ...

Q

Why did the Abyssinian turn on the radio?

A She wanted to relax to some mewsic.

JAIME: How did the cat beat the video game?

ROBERTO: He had nine lives!

Q

What do cats use for fresh breath?

A Mousewash.

SUPER SLEEPERS

THESE ARE JUST AVERAGES! SLEEPING HABITS FOR WILD ANIMALS ARE TRICKY TO TRACK.

The average domestic cat spends more than half of the day snoozing. Though they may look lazy, these sleepy kitties are just resting up for intense bursts of activity at dawn and dusk. That's when their ancestors did their hunting—and they needed all the energy they could get for it. Check out how some other animals' average daily sleeping times compare to those of catzzzzz.

Python
18 hours

Giraffe
1.9 hours

Human (adult)
8 hours

Domestic dog
10.6 hours

Domestic cat
12.1 hours

Brown bat
19.9 hours

Asian elephant
3.9 hours

Three-toed sloth
14.4 hours

Tiger
15.8 hours

FURGET IT!

Most calico and tortoiseshell cats are female, while most orange cats are male.

Some cat breeds have no (or almost no) fur. They have a variety of skin colors and patterns so they don't all look alike.

SOME PEOPLE USE **FUR SHED BY CATS TO CREATE CUTE CRAFTS.**
ONE ARTIST EVEN MADE HATS FROM THE HAIR HER KITTIES HAD SHED.

MANY CATS HAVE BLACK COLORING, BUT ONLY ONE BREED IS ALWAYS **BLACK: THE BOMBAY.**

MANY PEOPLE THINK THAT TABBY IS A BREED OF CAT, BUT THE TERM ACTUALLY DESCRIBES A DISTINCTIVE PATTERN IN A CAT'S COAT. TABBY CATS ARE FOUND IN MANY BREEDS. THEY TEND TO HAVE STRIPES, SPOTS, OR SWIRLS OF DIFFERENT-COLORED FUR.

Cats typically shed a little every day, but twice a year they go through a big shedding phase, called the exogen phase of fur growth. In the fall, it's to get ready for a new winter coat, and in the spring, it's to get rid of all the heavy hair.

Most cats have a double coat,
consisting of straighter, longer hairs known as guard hairs and an undercoat made of shorter, thicker hairs. A few breeds (such as the Siberian) have a triple coat, and some, like the Cornish rex, have only one!

Hairless cats may need an extra layer of warmth if it is cold outside, SO BUNDLE THEM UP!

SKIN IN THE GAME

Test your knowledge of cat parts with this larger-than-life quiz!

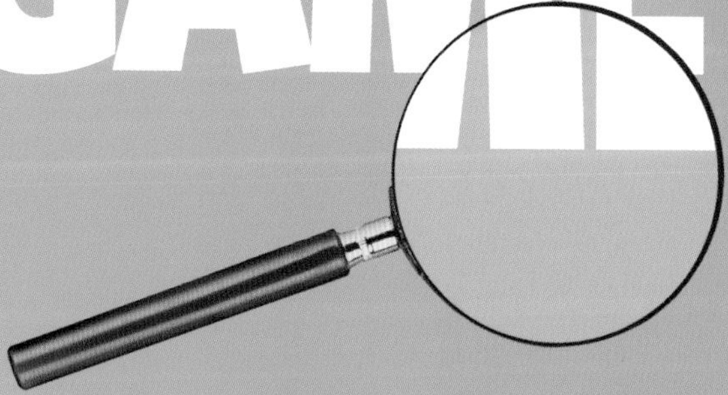

1

2

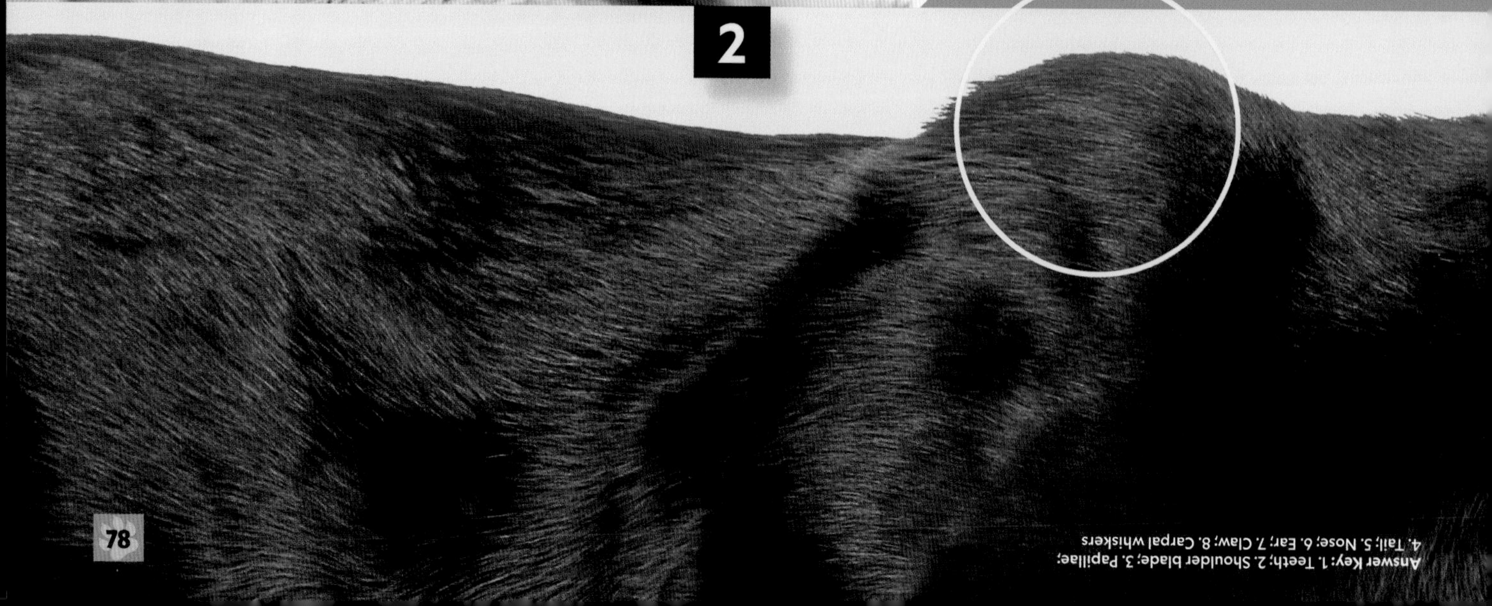

Answer Key: 1. Teeth; 2. Shoulder blade; 3. Papillae; 4. Tail; 5. Nose; 6. Ear; 7. Claw; 8. Carpal whiskers

LONG-DISTANCE TRAVELERS

IN 2013, BONNIE AND JACOB RICHTER FROM WEST PALM BEACH, FLORIDA, U.S.A., took their four-year-old tortoiseshell cat on vacation with them. The cat, Holly, had traveled with her owners before and was usually fine on trips. But this time, Holly got spooked by some loud noises, and she escaped the camper where the Richters were staying in Daytona Beach. After days of searching, the devastated couple had to return home without her.

HOLLY COMES HOME

Two months later, something incredible happened. A woman in West Palm Beach found a tired and hungry tortoiseshell cat in her backyard. A vet scanned the cat's microchip and confirmed that it was Holly. The cat had somehow trekked 190 miles (305 km) to make her way back home!

Holly was soon reunited with her owners. The Richters had no idea how their kitty had found her way, but they were thrilled.

And Holly isn't the only cat to pull off a seemingly unbelievable feat of navigation. In Australia, a cat named Howie once traveled for 12 months and more than 1,000 miles (1,600 km) to reunite with his family.

HOMING INSTINCT

Astonishing journeys like these aren't common. But they happen often enough to raise questions. How exactly do cats navigate long distances to find their way home—often through places they've never been before? Unfortunately, scientists don't have a good understanding of this ability. But one possibility is that cats are able to perceive Earth's magnetic field. This invisible field surrounds the planet and gets stronger or weaker depending on where you are. Humans need tools like compasses to detect it. But other animals, such as migrating birds and sea turtles, can sense it with their bodies and are known to use it as a guide.

Whatever their methods, cats do have a natural sense of direction. German scientists demonstrated this with a clever experiment back in 1954. They placed cats in a large, circular maze with multiple exits evenly spaced around it. Most of the cats didn't just escape the maze—they did so through the exits that faced the direction of their homes!

CATS' SUPER SENSE OF SMELL LIKELY HELPS THEM NAVIGATE LONG DISTANCES. IF THE AIR IN ONE DIRECTION SMELLS MORE LIKE HOME THAN THE OTHER DIRECTION, THAT'S PROBABLY THE WAY THEY'LL GO.

CATS OFTEN NEED SEVERAL WEEKS TO GET USED TO THEIR NEW HOME AFTER A MOVE. IF THEY GET OUTSIDE BEFORE THEY'VE ADJUSTED, THEY MAY TRY TO HEAD BACK TO THEIR FORMER HOME.

CATS DO NOT HAVE A

SWEET TOOTH!

SCIENTISTS HAVE FOUND THAT, UNLIKE HUMANS—WHO CAN TASTE

SOUR, BITTER, SALTY, AND SWEET—

CATS ARE MISSING THE

SPECIAL

PROTEIN

THAT ALLOWS THEM TO TASTE SWEET THINGS.

DID YOU KNOW THAT CATS ARE ESPECIALLY SENSITIVE TO BITTER FOODS? SCIENTISTS BELIEVE THIS IS TO PREVENT THEM FROM EATING TOXIC THINGS IN THEIR ENVIRONMENT, WHICH OFTEN HAVE A BITTER TASTE.

NOT QUITE NIGHT VISION

EVER SEEN A CAT RACING FRANTICALLY AROUND THE HOUSE BETWEEN DINNER AND BEDTIME?

When cats get "the zoomies" at this hour, they're just following their instincts. Like their wild ancestors, cats are crepuscular animals. This means they're naturally most active around dawn and dusk. There isn't much light outside at these times, which would make hunting difficult for a daytime creature. Luckily for cats, their eyes are optimized for seeing during these dimly lit parts of the day.

SEEING DOUBLE

The basic structure of a cat's eye is similar to a human's. But a cat's is fine-tuned to soak up as much light as possible at night. A cat's pupils can dilate, or open, much wider than ours do. This lets extra light into the retina, the light-sensing structure at the back of the eye. A cat's retina has more light-absorbing cells, called rods, than a human's. This makes it much easier for a cat to detect things in low light.

Cats also have something we don't: a thin, shiny layer of tissue behind the retina. It's called the tapetum lucidum, which means "tapestry of light." This layer reflects light back for a second pass over the retina. The rod cells then get another shot at sensing the light and sending important visual information to the kitty's brain.

COLOR COMPROMISE

All in all, cats can see in the dark about six times better than humans do. But their night-vision powers come at a cost. Because their retinas have so many rod cells, cats have fewer cones—the cells that let us perceive color. This means that kitties see the world in different shades than humans do—but scientists aren't completely sure about which shades. This can also make it difficult for cats to make out objects that aren't moving. But the second you start wiggling that feather toy, you'd better believe a cat's eyes are on the case!

IN ADDITION TO DILATING IN DIM LIGHT, A CAT'S PUPILS WIDEN WHEN SOMETHING EXCITING OR SCARY IS HAPPENING. GOTTA STAY ALERT!

THAT'S HISSTERICAL!

KNOCK, KNOCK.

Who's there?
Purr.
Purr who?
One purrfect kitty!

Q What kind of cat can disappear?

A A meowgician.

Q What kind of stickers do cats use to decorate?

A Scratch and sniff!

Q What did the cat say to the love of his life?

A "Let's get meowied."

Q Why did the cat get sent to detention?

A She had a bad cattitude.

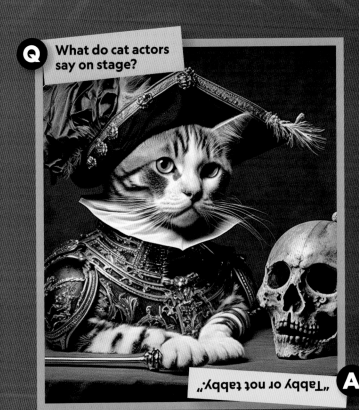

Q What do cat actors say on stage?

A "Tabby or not tabby."

Q What did the rock kitty say when his guitar was broken

A can't pawform in ese conditions!"

A SIGHT FOR SORE EYES

Have you noticed that when cats are acting playful **or they're afraid, their eyes get big and round? When cats are** excited, **they open their eyes wide and their pupils enlarge.**

Cats can't actually see in complete **darkness.** While their eyesight is much better than the average human's, they **do need some light** to see.

The rarest eye color for cats is COPPER. Most felines have lighter eye colors LIKE YELLOW, BLUE, OR GREEN. In humans, the most common color is brown—only 2 percent of people have green eyes!

Have you ever seen a cat's pupil, or center of their eyes, go from a big black circle to just a narrow slit when you turn on a light or open a window? This is to protect their eyes and filter out light so that they can see. Humans do this too, but it is much less noticeable.

MELANIN IS A PIGMENT THAT PROVIDES COLOR TO **SKIN, HAIR, AND EYES.** BUT CATS (AND OTHER ANIMALS) WITH BLUE EYES DON'T HAVE ANY MELANIN IN THEIR EYES— THEIR EYES ARE ACTUALLY CLEAR! WE SEE THEM AS BLUE BECAUSE OF THE **REFLECTION OF LIGHT.**

Cat eyes appear to **glow in the dark** because of a reflective surface on their eyes called tapetum lucidum. This special surface reflects light and helps cats **see better in the dark.**

CATS CAN SEE THINGS THAT ARE **CLOSER TO THEM** BETTER THAN THEY CAN SEE THINGS THAT ARE FAR AWAY. **THEIR WHISKERS** HELP THEM "SEE" (OR SENSE) OBJECTS THAT ARE SUPER CLOSE TO THEIR FACES.

Humans can see more colors than cats.

SINGAPURA CATS ARE KNOWN FOR THEIR **HUGE ROUND EYES.**

Turn the page for more facts about cat eyes!

Cat eyes can track objects faster than a **human's eyes** can. This is why cats are great at **hunting fast-moving rodents** or toys.

The nutrient taurine is essential to cats' **eye health.** It's found in chicken, fish, and beef. Although some other mammals—like humans and dogs—can produce taurine naturally, cats cannot. This is why it's **very important** for meat to be included in their diets.

Some cats—and humans—can have a rare trait called **heterochromia** that causes them to have two distinct eye colors.

Cats can see a wider view than humans can. While the average human has a 180-degree view, cats have a 200-degree view.

Most cats don't like direct eye contact. Some even view it as aggressive or threatening.

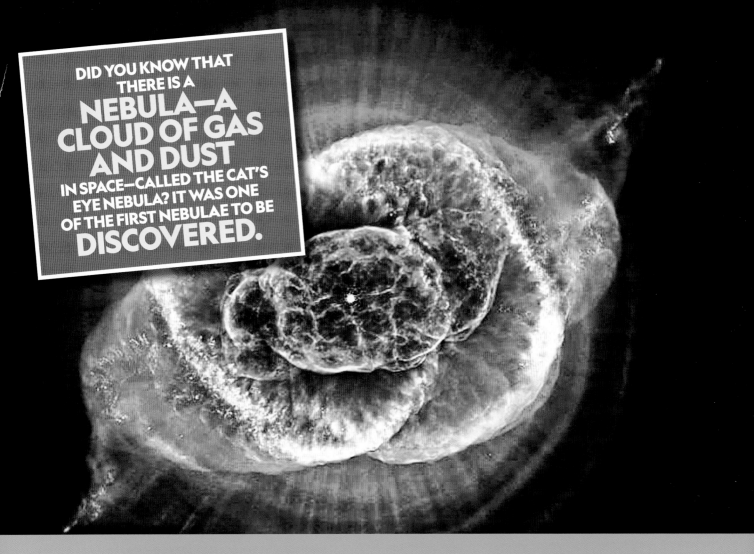

DID YOU KNOW THAT THERE IS A NEBULA—A CLOUD OF GAS AND DUST IN SPACE—CALLED THE CAT'S EYE NEBULA? IT WAS ONE OF THE FIRST NEBULAE TO BE **DISCOVERED.**

A cat's pupils **adjust faster** than a human's, allowing them to **adapt to light change** faster.

CATS WITH BLUE EYES AND WHITE FUR ARE MORE LIKELY TO BE **DEAF.**

CAT COMEDY

KNOCK, KNOCK.

Who's there?
Theodore.
Theodore who?
The-o-door doesn't have a cat flap, so I'm going to need you to open it!

Q What did the cat chef make for dinner?

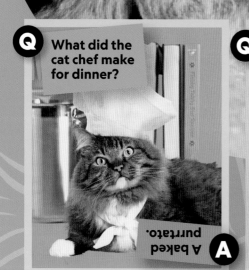

A A baked purrtato.

Q What do you call a backpack that a cat likes to curl up on?

A A napsack.

Q Do cats like running in a straight line?

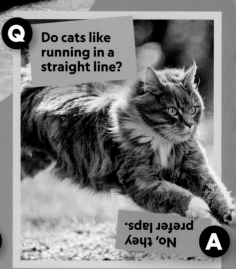

A No, they prefer laps.

BACK to SCHOOL

LAUGHABLE LIST

A cat's favorite artists:

Frida Pawhlo

....

Jean-Michel Basquicat

....

Edvard Mewnch

....

CAT 1: What's your favorite class in school?
CAT 2: Probably world hisstory.
CAT 1: Oh, really? Mine is pee-E!

KNOCK, KNOCK.

Who's there?
Neil!
Neil who?
Neil down and
pet this cat!

FURMIDABLE FACTS

Test your feline vocab by matching the words on the left with their definitions on the right. (Hint: You can find all these terms explained somewhere in this book.)

1

TAPETUM LUCIDUM

2

RETINA

3

DOMESTICATE

4

VESTIBULAR SYSTEM

5

CREPUSCULAR

6

VIBRISSAE

7

PAPILLAE

8

NICTITATING MEMBRANE

9

RETRACT

A

To tame an animal as a pet or for use on a farm

B

An inner eyelid that keeps a cat's eyes moist and clean

C

The hundreds of sharp, backward-facing keratin spines on a cat tongue

D

A reflective surface that causes the eyes of animals to look like they are glowing in the dark. Many species of nocturnal animals have this layer in their eyes.

E

A specialized type of hair that helps cats sense things

F

To pull in

G

Being most active at dawn and dusk

H

The internal parts of a cat's body that help it balance and right itself

I

The light-sensing structure at the back of the eye

Answer Key: 1. D; 2. I; 3. A; 4. H; 5. G; 6. E; 7. C; 8. B; 9. F.

95

STUDYING CATTITUDES

KRISTYN VITALE, CAT BEHAVIORIST

Kristyn Vitale is a scientist who specializes in studying cat social behavior. She designs experiments to help understand how cats interact with each other and how they think. Here, she describes her research and the surprising things she's learned about the social lives of cats.

WHAT MADE YOU DECIDE TO STUDY THE SOCIAL BEHAVIOR OF CATS?

A lot of people have this idea that cats are aloof and don't really care about us. But growing up with cats, that wasn't my experience at all. I felt like our family cats were seeking out attention. It's true that other members of the feline family are solitary in nature, but that doesn't mean domestic cats are, because they've spent so much more time around people. The more research we conduct, the more we're seeing that social interaction is actually a really important part of cats' lives.

WHAT HAVE YOU LEARNED ABOUT HOW CATS FEEL ABOUT PEOPLE?

My colleagues and I did a study to find out what kind of bonds cats have with their owners. We had the owners bring their cats into an unfamiliar space—our lab—and we watched how the cats reacted to being left alone there. Most cats would just sit by the door and meow a lot. But when the owners returned, the cats would calm down and start to explore more. This told us that—for the majority of cats—their owners are a source of comfort and reassurance in stressful situations.

In another experiment, we gave cats a choice. We put them on the floor an equal distance away from a person, a food they liked, a toy they liked, and something that smelled interesting, like catnip. Surprisingly, half of the cats chose to go interact with the person—even when their favorite food was right there!

HOW CAN PET OWNERS FORM CLOSER RELATIONSHIPS WITH THEIR CATS?

If you want to connect with a cat, finding out what they like is really important. Give the cat a choice between different food items and different toys. Play with them, pet them, brush them, and see which activity they stay engaged with for the longest time. Those are the things your cat enjoys!

FELINE FEELINGS

Cats don't show much emotion on their faces. But they have other ways of telling people and fellow animals how they feel. Body language is one of the primary ways that cats communicate with each other—and with us. Check out some of the different ways cats can express themselves using their tails, ears, whiskers, and other body parts.

Mood: Friendly

Body language: Whiskers forward, ears in a natural position, approaching with the tail upright. This cat is coming to say hello!

Mood: Relaxed

Body language: Lying on side with the belly visible, eyes partly or all the way closed. This cat feels safe enough to let its guard down.

Mood: Playful

Body language: Eyes wide open, ears pointing forward, often standing up straight with the tail curved over the back or leaning back with front paws extended. This kitty is ready for adventure.

Mood: Nervous

Body language: Eyes wide open, ears swiveled sideways, crouching slightly with the tail held close to the body. This kitty is in a protective position and prepared to react.

Mood: Frightened

Body language: Whiskers back, ears flattened, crouching all the way down with the tail tucked between the legs. This cat is trying to look nonthreatening in hopes of avoiding a fight.

Mood: Annoyed

Body language: Eyes open, ears swiveled sideways, tail twitching or waving back and forth. Time to leave this kitty alone!

Mood: Angry

Body language: Whiskers back, ears flattened, arching back with the legs stiffened and the body and tail fur puffing out. This cat is trying to look as large as possible to intimidate its foe.

MULTIPURPOSE PAWS

THERE'S NO DOUBT ABOUT IT: CAT PAWS ARE ADORABLE.
Those furry feet and squishy toe beans seem like they were designed to melt our hearts. But the features of a cat's paw aren't just there to win us over. They all have useful functions that helped cats' wild ancestors survive.

PURRFECT PADDING
Cats' paw pads are one of the only places on their bodies without fur on them. (The tip of the nose is another one.) The hairless skin helps keep kitties from slipping while they walk and is extremely sensitive to touch. The pads are filled with fatty tissue, which helps absorb shock when a cat completes one of its epic jumps. The squishiness also makes cats' footsteps nearly silent—that's important when they're stalking prey.

Some long-haired breeds have tufts of hair growing in between their individual toe pads. For cats that originated in colder areas, these crops of hair were crucial for gaining traction on snow. In cats' domesticated lives, though, this adaptation isn't always relevant. In fact, some kitties need this toe hair trimmed so they don't slide around on hardwood floors.

CLAWS OUT
Cats' claws are another essential element for their survival. Claws help cats hunt, climb, and defend themselves from attack. Like hooves and fingernails, claws are made of a tough material called keratin. But unlike our fingernails, which grow out of our skin, a cat's claws are connected directly to its foot bones. To extend its claws, a cat flexes its foot, pushing the claws out from their sheaths in between the paw pads. This motion also spreads out the toes, which increases the width of the foot and can help the cat grab wriggling prey.

Scratching on a vertical surface helps cats relieve stress and keeps their claws ready for action. The more they scratch, the pointier their claw tips get, like sharpening a pencil. Scratching also keeps the claws clean and removes any loose layers of keratin. Just make sure there are plenty of scratching posts around, because as far as a cat is concerned, the arm of the couch would work just as well!

THAT'S HISSTERICAL!

KNOCK, KNOCK.

Who's there?
The vet.
Uh, nobody's home! Go away!

Q How do you spell mousetrap in just three letters?

A C-A-T.

Q Why was the cat fired as the security guard from the pillow factory?

SECURITY

A He was caught taking a catnap.

Q Why do cats always get good Christmas presents?

A Because they are good friends with Santa Claws.

Q What do you call a cat that's just eaten beans?

A Puss 'n' Toots.

Q What animal has more lives than a cat?

A A frog, because it croaks every night and still wakes up the next morning!

KNOCK, KNOCK.

Who's there?
Furry.
Furry who?
Your Furry Godmother! It's time to go to the ball!

CATS VS. HUMANS

According to **scientists,** cats may think of humans they are fond of as **big hairless cats.**

Did you know that some cats can learn to open doors just like humans? It's easier for them to open door handles with levers ... but some cats have learned to turn doorknobs, too!

JUST LIKE HUMAN NAILS, A CAT'S CLAWS **CONTINUE GROWING THROUGHOUT ITS LIFE.**

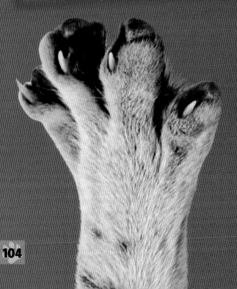

THE PATTERN ON EACH CAT'S NOSE IS UNIQUE—SORT OF LIKE A HUMAN'S FINGERPRINTS.

Kittens meow to their mothers to let them know when they are hungry or cold. But once they grow up, cats usually stop meowing to each other. Meowing is something adult cats mostly do for humans; it's a special language for communicating with us!

A cat's heartbeat is about twice as fast AS A HUMAN'S.

Ever wondered what makes a cat so stealthy? While humans put their heels down first when walking, cats put their TOES DOWN FIRST. This puts less pressure on the ground and allows them to move silently.

EXPERTS THINK THAT CATS PROBABLY DREAM ABOUT THE THINGS THAT HAPPEN DURING THE DAY AND PEOPLE THEY KNOW. THAT MEANS A CAT PROBABLY DREAMS ABOUT ITS OWNERS!

CRAZY ABOUT CATS

C ats live all around the globe, and so do the people who love them. This means that felines have been featured in the art, theater, and popular culture of many societies. This map shows some of the different ways people have paid tribute to cats throughout the world, from thousands of years ago to today.

What: Internet cat videos

Where: Spokane, Washington, U.S.A.

Fun Facts: In 1984, a man named Charlie Schmidt made a video of his orange cat "playing" the piano. When the man uploaded it to YouTube 23 years later, it became one of the world's first viral cat videos.

Spokane,
Washington,
U.S.A.
NORTH AMERICA

ATLANTIC OCEAN

SOUTH AMERICA

Nasca,
PERU

PACIFIC OCEAN

What: Cat mummies

Where: Egypt

Fun Facts: More than 3,000 years ago, ancient Egyptians considered cats a sacred species. People kept cats in their homes, adorned them with jewelry, and sometimes even shared food off the same plate! And this reverence didn't end when a cat died. Many Egyptian royals had their pets mummified to accompany them into the afterlife.

What: Enormous cat etching

Where: Nasca, Peru

Fun Facts: In 2020, archaeologists unearthed this larger-than-life line drawing of a cat etched into a hillside in southern Peru. The cat measures about 120 feet (37 m) from end to end and is one of hundreds of gigantic images thought to be made by Indigenous Nasca and Paracas people more than 2,000 years ago.

What: *CATS* the musical

Where: London, England, UK

Fun Facts: This fantastical show by Andrew Lloyd Webber premiered in London in 1981 and New York City the next year. Since then, it has been performed in more than 30 countries and been seen by more than 75 million people. Actors dressed as colorful cats prowl and strut across the stage, singing about their lives and troubles.

ARCTIC OCEAN

London, U.K.

EUROPE

Istanbul, TURKEY

ASIA

JAPAN

PACIFIC OCEAN

EGYPT

AFRICA

INDIAN OCEAN

AUSTRALIA

NEW ZEALAND

What: Cozy cat houses

Where: Istanbul, Turkey

Fun Facts: For thousands of years, stray cats have wandered the streets of Turkey's largest city, Istanbul. Residents consider the free-roaming animals communal pets—and helpful rat hunters. Some even build mini houses on the sidewalks to keep the city kitties warm and dry.

GALIT & BESUTU TARAFINDAN YAPTIRILMISTIR

What: Giant cat murals

Where: New Zealand

Fun Facts: Street artist Mikal Carter paints realistic cat murals on the side of buildings in his home country of New Zealand. Each painting depicts a real stray cat that has found or is looking for its furever home.

What: Maneki-neko, or lucky cats

Where: Japan

Fun Facts: These cute cat figurines often greet customers entering Japanese stores and restaurants. One paw is raised in a gesture meant to beckon people inside. The statues, which are based on Japanese bobtail cats, are thought to bring good fortune to a business.

COOL COATS

A cat's coat can come in many different patterns and colors, from spotted to striped and fluffy to sleek. Take a look at these just-for-fun records of the coolest—and cutest—coats around.

MOST UNUSUAL COAT

DONSKOY

The honors for most unusual coat go to a cat with no coat at all. Donskoy cats are almost completely bald, thanks to a harmless genetic mutation. These cute kitties require bathing or wiping down to keep their skin healthy. Donskoys are friendly, intelligent, and energetic.

SPOTTIEST COAT

BENGAL

The Bengal is known for having one of the spottiest coats—similar to those sported by their leopard cousins. These cats need lots of play and exercise, and some Bengals have been known to retrieve items like dogs. They are also one of the few cat breeds that enjoy playing in water.

MOST COLORFUL COAT

CALICO CATS

Calico isn't a breed; it's a type of coloring that includes at least three colors: black, orange, and white. It can occur across several breeds, including American shorthairs, Japanese bobtails, and Siberians.

WARMEST COAT

SIBERIAN

The award for the fluffiest coat (though there is some stiff—or should we say, soft—competition!) goes to the Siberian. This cat breed is known for its incredibly thick coat. These fabulous felines are also famed for their cuddles and laid-back personalities.

STRIPIEST COAT

DRAGON LI

While there are many different striped cats, the Dragon Li breed (also known as the Chinese Li Hua) from China is known for the many striking stripes on its coat, making it one of the stripiest cats around! Dragon Lis love the outdoors and excel at hunting. Owners should make sure these independent cats have plenty of space to roam and explore.

ALL EARS

WHEN A KITTEN IS BORN, IT CAN'T HEAR OR SEE. BUT AT AROUND ONE WEEK, A KITTEN'S EAR CANALS OPEN, ALLOWING IT TO HEAR THE OUTSIDE WORLD.

Cats that are born deaf can learn how to **communicate with their owners** in different ways, including through **SIGN LANGUAGE** or the use of laser pointers.

Cats can move EACH EAR up to 180 degrees.

CATS CAN MOVE THEIR EARS IN THE DIRECTION OF A SOUND TO INCREASE THEIR HEARING ABILITY BY ABOUT **15 TO 20 PERCENT.**

Many cats can't stand the sound of televisions. This is because they can hear high-frequency noises that humans can't.

A CAT'S HEARING is better than a **DOG'S.** While dogs do have great hearing, **CATS** can hear lower and higher frequencies.

In one study, SCIENTISTS CREATED SONGS specially designed for feline hearing—**AND THE CATS LOVED THEM!**

Studies show that a cat can recognize its OWNER'S VOICE.

PURRFECT PITCH

FOR A DOMESTIC CAT, PURRING IS THE ULTIMATE SIGN OF HAPPINESS. It's basically the feline equivalent of a dog wagging its tail! Cats learn to purr as tiny kittens, when they're still nursing from their mothers. It is thought that the low, rumbly sound helps kittens locate their mother at feeding time. Many adult cats purr when they are fed—or when they think they're about to be fed. Cats might also purr when they're playing, when people pet them, or when they're settling down to sleep.

HOW IT WORKS

When a cat feels the urge to purr, its brain sends a signal to the throat muscles. The cat's larynx, or voice box, starts bending and flexing to flutter the folds of its vocal cords (the part of the body that helps create noise for communication). The vocal cords then start vibrating super quickly. As the cat's breath flows past them, it creates sound waves that carry the sound of the purr

through the air. Think of it like sticking your tongue out and blowing air past it to make a *plllffftttt* noise. But if you were purring, you'd be using your throat to do it instead of your lips and tongue.

Most cat vocalizations, like meowing, can only happen as a cat breathes out. But purring continues as they inhale, too, for an uninterrupted soothing sound.

GOOD VIBRATIONS

Purring is most often considered a sign of contentment. But cats also purr in stressful situations, such as when they're injured or upset. Some scientists have suggested that the vibrations of purring actually promote healing and bone growth, helping cats recover more quickly. It's also possible that simply breathing deeply to purr helps kitties calm themselves, the same way taking a few deep breaths can help humans relax.

BEFORE SCIENTISTS LEARNED THAT THE LARYNX IS INVOLVED IN PURRING, PEOPLE THOUGHT THE SOUND CAME FROM BLOOD RUSHING THROUGH A CAT'S VEINS TO ITS HEART.

BOBCATS, CHEETAHS, AND COUGARS CAN ALL PURR. LIONS AND TIGERS, HOWEVER, CANNOT.

CAT COMEDY

KNOCK, KNOCK.

Who's there?
Les.
Les who?
Les go inside, that's where the cat food is!

Q At what time is a cat most likely to use the litter box?

A Pee o'clock!

Q What do kittens wear?

A Diapurrs!

TONGUE TWISTER

SAY THIS FAST THREE TIMES:

Paws plodded purposefully upon the puffy purple carpet.

CAT ARTIST 1: Behold! I've finished my meowsterpiece.

CAT ARTIST 2: That's beautiful! No—it's purrfect.

YOU'VE CAT TO BE KITTEN ME ...

Q Why was the kitten's voice so quiet?

A Because she was just whiskering.

Q What breakfast cereal do cats love the most?

A Mice Krispies!

TUNA TRAP

Your cat wants dinner, but you are comfy on the couch and not in the mood to get up. Kitty tries rubbing up against your legs and purring. No luck. He tries meowing. You still don't get the hint, so he moves to a loud *yoowwl!* A few yowls like that and you're willing to get up, just to stop the noise. Next time, he'll know that loud yowling is the way to go. That's learning. You can test your cat's ability to learn by giving him a puzzle and seeing if he can solve it faster with practice.

STEP 1:

Show your cat the tuna and place it in one of the holes in the muffin tin. Cover the hole with the Wiffle ball. The holes in the Wiffle ball will allow your cat to see and smell the tuna.

YOU WILL NEED:

SMALL CLUMP OF TUNA OR ANY OF YOUR CAT'S FAVORITE SMELLY TREATS

MUFFIN TIN

A SMALL PLASTIC BALL, SUCH AS A WIFFLE BALL

CLOCK OR TIMER

PAPER AND PENCIL OR PEN

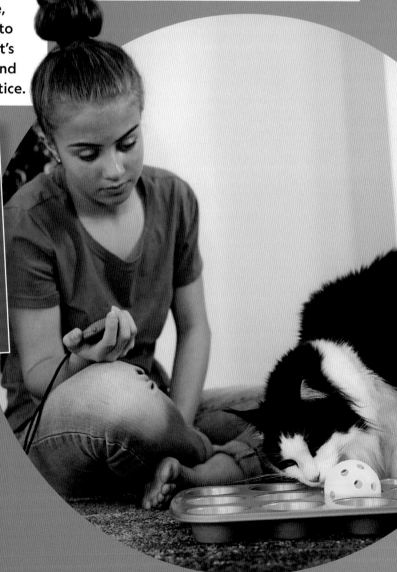

NEVER FORCE A CAT TO DO ANYTHING THEY DON'T WANT TO DO. IF THEY AREN'T INTERESTED IN THE EXPERIMENT, YOU CAN ALWAYS TRY AGAIN LATER!

STEP 2:

Time how long it takes your cat to move the ball and get the tuna.

STEP 3:

Repeat the process three more times. Record how long it takes him to get the tuna each time.

STEP 4:

Compare the times. If your cat was faster on his second, third, and fourth tries, it shows that he learned how to extract the tuna quickly.

CONCLUSION:

If you were given a delicious treat trapped in a muffin tin, you'd look at the setup and see that you need to pick up the ball and grab the treat. Scientists say when you can study a problem and design a solution, you have insight. Your cat has a harder time. He has to discover, step-by-step, how to get the tuna. He might try pushing down on the ball with his nose, or look to you for help. Eventually, he'll use his nose or paw to push the ball aside. When he sees the same setup again, he has to remember: Out of all the things he did last time, which one got him the chance to chow down? Scientists call this learning by trial and error. Your cat doesn't care what you call it. He's only in it for the treats!

THE
GENETIC CONDITION
THAT MAKES A
CHIMERA CAT
CAN OCCUR IN ANY DOMESTIC CAT,
WHICH IS WHY
CHIMERAS
AREN'T A BREED.

A CHIMERA CAT CAN HAVE A DIFFERENT COLOR ON EACH SIDE OF ITS FACE OR BODY—SOMETIMES SPLIT IN A STRAIGHT LINE DOWN THE MIDDLE! THIS IS BECAUSE A CHIMERA CAT HAS TWO SETS OF DNA, WHILE MOST ANIMALS ONLY HAVE ONE. DNA IS THE MATERIAL INSIDE ALL LIVING THINGS THAT DETERMINES HOW AN ORGANISM WILL LOOK AND BEHAVE.

EAR ME OUT

Can you get a purrfect score on these feline comprehension questions? Write your answers on a separate piece of paper and then check them against the answer key. If you're stumped, review the second half of this book for some clues.

1. When do cats purr?
a. when they are happy
b. when they receive food
c. when they are in stressful situations
d. all of the above

2. Which of these animals cannot purr?
a. cheetahs
b. lions
c. bobcats
d. cougars

3. True or False? Cats are crepuscular animals.

4. The rarest eye color for cats is?
a. copper
b. yellow
c. blue
d. green

5. True or False? A human heart beats faster than a cat's.

6. Which continent has conditions too harsh for domestic cats to survive outdoors?
a. Africa
b. Antarctica
c. Europe
d. Asia

Answer Key: 1. d; 2. b; 3. True. Cats are most active at dusk and dawn. 4. c; 5. False. A cat's heart beats twice as fast as a human's. 6. b; 7. c; 8. d; 9. a; 10. False. Cats are unable to taste sweet things.

7. **What does it mean when a cat arches its back and flattens its ears?**
   a. It thinks something is really funny!
   b. It's gassy and needs to let it out.
   c. It's nervous.
   d. It's happy.

8. **Which of these is the name of a pattern of coat—not a cat breed?**
   a. Bengal
   b. Tabby
   c. Calico
   d. Both b and c

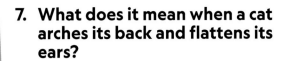

9. **What is taurine?**
   a. an essential nutrient cats need for their eyes
   b. a favorite snack of cats
   c. a cat's favorite rock band
   d. a famous cat hotel

10. **True or False? Cats can taste sweet things.**

BREED PRONUNCIATION GUIDE

HERE'S HOW TO PRONOUNCE THE CAT BREEDS FEATURED IN THIS BOOK.

A
Abyssinian: AB-uh-SIN-ee-in
American bobtail: uh-MARE-ih-ken BOB-tail
American shorthair: uh-MARE-ih-ken SHORT-hair
Australian mist: ah-STRAYL-yen MIST

B
Bengal: BEN-gul
Bombay: bom-BAY
Brazilian shorthair: bruh-ZIL-yen SHORT-hair

C
Chartreux: sharr-TROOS

D
Donskoy: DONS-koy
Dragon Li: DRAG-un LEE

E
Egyptian mau: ee-JIP-shun MOW

J
Japanese bobtail: JAP-uh-NEES BOB-tail

M
Maine coon cat: MANE COON CAT
Manx: MANKS

N
Norwegian forest cat: nor-WEE-jun FOR-ist cat

P
Persian: PUR-zhun

R
Ragdoll: RAG-doll
Russian blue: RUSH-un BLOO

S
Scottish fold: SKAA-tish FOHLD
Selkirk rex: SEL-kerk RECKS
Siamese: SIE-uh-meez
Siberian: sie-BEE-ree-uhn
Singapura: SING-uh-POR-uh
Somali: suh-MAA-lee
Sphynx: SFINGKS

T
Turkish Van: TUR-kish VAN

INDEX

CREDITS

ACKNOWLEDGMENTS

TO ZADIE, THE WORLD'S SMARTEST, WEIRDEST CAT. —M. G.
TO THE DAD WHO TAUGHT ME CURIOSITY AND THE KIDS WHO KEEP IT ALIVE. —B. M.

Since 1888, the National Geographic Society has funded more than 14,000 research, conservation, education, and storytelling projects around the world. National Geographic Partners distributes a portion of the funds it receives from your purchase to National Geographic Society to support programs including the conservation of animals and their habitats. To learn more, visit natgeo.com/info.

For more information, visit nationalgeographic.com, call 1-877-873-6846, or write to the following address:

National Geographic Partners, LLC
1145 17th Street NW
Washington, DC 20036-4688 U.S.A.

For librarians and teachers: nationalgeographic.com/books/librarians-and-educators

More for kids from National Geographic: natgeokids.com

National Geographic Kids magazine inspires children to explore their world with fun yet educational articles on animals, science, nature, and more. Using fresh storytelling and amazing photography, *Nat Geo Kids* shows kids ages 6 to 14 the fascinating truth about the world—and why they should care. **natgeo.com/subscribe**

For rights or permissions inquiries, please contact National Geographic Books Subsidiary Rights: bookrights@natgeo.com

Designed by Waterbury Publications, Inc.

Trade paperback ISBN: 978-1-4263-7590-3
Reinforced library binding ISBN: 978-1-4263-7592-7

The publisher would like to acknowledge Teresa Keiger, allbreed judge, Cat Fanciers' Association, and Alicia Klepeis, fact-checker, for their expert review. Thanks also to Brett Challos, design manager; Sarah J. Mock, senior photo editor; Alison O'Brien Muff, photo editor; Paige Towler, project manager; Emily Fego, project editor; Mike McNey, map production; Michael J. Horner, map edit; and Lauren Sciortino and David Marvin, associate designers.

Printed in China
23/PPS/1